HOW NARROW MY ESCAPES

HOW NARROW MY ESCAPES

❊

LILLIAN-YVONNE BERTRAM

NEW MICHIGAN PRESS
TUCSON, ARIZONA

NEW MICHIGAN PRESS
DEPT OF ENGLISH, P. O. BOX 210067
UNIVERSITY OF ARIZONA
TUCSON, AZ 85721-0067

<http://newmichiganpress.com>

Orders and queries to <nmp@thediagram.com>.

Copyright © 2019 by Lillian-Yvonne Bertram.
All rights reserved.

ISBN 978-1-934832-71-4. FIRST PRINTING.

Printed in the United States of America.

Design by Ander Monson.

Cover art by Laylah Ali
Untitled from "Greenheads series."
Gouache on paper. 2003.
© Laylah Ali

CONTENTS

If in its advance the plague begins to fiercen   1
Miracle Cure   2
How Narrow My Escapes   3
My Past Has Value   7
Raise her dark matter   9
Netherland   11
"They were armed with long guns"   13
I believe the far fields are made of glass   25
Negative Money   26
I often fall asleep with one earring in my ear   28
Maine Coast   29
Facts About Deer   30
Husband Stories   32
Georgic   36

Acknowledgments   39

IF IN ITS ADVANCE THE PLAGUE BEGINS TO FIERCEN

Virgil

Tomorrow you will be stung by a bee.
Tonight a cute boy lays his cock on your
hi. You invite him to your no. You invite his cock
To no it down. And if you are not doing This. And if you are not
Doing That. What do you invite him to turn to. In?
You invite what slumber mutely passes for.
Sheet fisted into balls. The cross hatchings of your pattern
Stunned into forever shuns. Oh. So this is how
I towel throw. So tricky. Throat what little. Left of
The blithe night is the right thing you did not turn
Soon enough to hook. This mistook won't be forgiven.
Misdeeds booked by whom? Tomorrow you will be stung
By a bee. It will kill you. You will die into
The hard pit of a date.

MIRACLE CURE: A CAST SPELL

What I know about severed heads:
    tongues do not float away to join
    angelic choirs. Tongues rot like
    tongues and eyes cure into mica.
I was driven to survive unloaded. Down
    there see the salmon run, men holed up
    at the mouth, in the rush to feed.
    I toss them moonlit flesh without even
being asked! Now you see me, now you
    see me bolt my foot to this floor.
    Thankless men burn my dead so lazily.
    The kingdom of God, they say,
is the cunt that locked you out. I will live
    past whatever I can. The right half of me
    is on fever. A man I am not fucking
    cautions me against unsanctioned hot
springs. *Don't boil to death* is such succulent devotion.
    God bless those who fully escape. I skinnydip
    past men at the mouth thronging to feed.
    I love their filth and all their bursting veins.

HOW NARROW MY ESCAPES

I may still have been

a girl then & a cheap
      drunk watching opossums
molest another

harvest weekend.

      I went two years with no
sex. For this the boys

declared me leaf or

      cutting, plant planted
to grow not needing it.

No one knew

where to look for me
      but who was ever looking.

I staged my portraits:

      hung myself, neck out
of view, a shade

in the making.
>	In the long exposures
I clinched my flimsy

shadow,
>	us doubled up in the stupid
shirtdress

that never fit

>	my hips, kitten heels I'd one
day vomit on

in Brooklyn,
>	just like a real girl. Please
don't tell

my mother
>	what she already knows—I
had to

reinvent the well,
>	dedicate each spade's heap
to the starry

bottom and there

    you'll find me still,
dreaming that rain

follows the plow.

    Did I year wrong? My student
tells me

we are in the *last days,*

    that God will pour out his
seven bowls

of Armageddon,
    just punishment for the
wicked. *The end*

of the world is near,
    he says, *look around and*
you will see the prophecy

fulfilled.
    I look around & see
that making it on merit

is a wooden
    nickel and my cup
of wine is filled with holy

air. I kept

    the mouse-killing cat
& tonight

he watches me

    floss so greedily I bleed. Did
you not know

that to anoint

    someone your last love is to
tempt them

to flight?
    Alone I drink and drink
under my cracked

lacquered
    tiles of pride. Whole days I
send this tongue

around my teeth
    but nothing gives up its
hiding place.

Once, I had two dreams:
    one *lazy*, the other, *away*.

MY PAST HAS VALUE

to the men who never knew me
then. If pretty now, think how pretty when
so newly wounded in a world.
They paid for rent,
spent hundreds in rare steaks on birthdays;
shined my blackest eyes
to wandering pearls.
                Men away from wives
on work trips are simple men
with simpler desires. Did I remind them
of someone they never netted
& spoiled? To the first man who checked
me in the corner bookshop at thirteen
& left ten dollars at the counter
for that girl —thank you
                for Vonnegut, Bukowski,
                and Freud. Men
on the shelf of men who tell me
what to think, men who toyed
with drunk too much, drive too reckless,
who interpret for me
all my dreams.

To the man who said I was too much
hyperbola—you were right.
    To the night
car salesman who let me test-drive
to Whole Foods, paid for my cashews
—thank you, you fool
for the boyfriend who made me walk
on the inside. Too easy for a girl to get meloned:
flesh scooped up & out.
    As for the first
husband, all his likenesses stowed in family albums
I snuck out and composted
with dirtied dresses. I've clammed up & now nothing
here to test his existence.
     Husband, what did I leave you for
and what became of those many-named
goldfish so elaborately poured down the drain?
   As for you, father, you always had a thing
for fairness &
better-floating boats. Thank you for knowing
    the marina was the safest place
to take me as a child, where I skipped
rocks, learned to pace myself on the fickle docks,
and admire the sleepy teak-decked tombs
       of other people's money.

RAISE HER DARK MATTER

Come witness my cunt
made of deer meat

my drying
dry throat. Men

motorcycle by
the lakeside & behold

I glide as gravel
to the shore,

issue a magic trick.
I raise my dark matter

to the height of kites
cooly strung about

the sky, lie
my stone back

to the rough island.
A fiddle whine

or whistle
interrupts my sun-

spanked day.
This new shadow

above me is the sweat-
salted face

of someone's child—
boy or girl

it doesn't matter.
I curse and

it bursts into doves.

NETHERLAND

The czar and his children
all burnt. Rib

cage of coal
flowers. Script

faxed by accuser
to accused. Grandfather

did or did not
hammer at the Reich,

his acts lost to Parkinson's
last memory.

After he crossed
the bridge, the bridge

was bombed. A country

sunk once again.
How many the boats

of the dead float
up in the flood.

Grandfather pages
through the faces

of that town:
the miller, the baker

the candlestick
maker. Gone gone

gone. Their houses
their fields

their children all burnt.

"THEY WERE ARMED WITH LONG GUNS"

1)

and that's how everyone they shot, died.

2)

    Some sin turns
its silver key. You know

    where this
is going. This is

    America. Nothing innocent
about them fallen leaves,

    nothing innocent
about this family tree.

3)

I fear going to_____ (circle all that apply):

- Federal buildings
- Consulates
- Shopping malls
- Concert venues
- Post offices
- McDonald's
- Stadiums
- Parties
- Subway stations
- Marathons
- Rallies
- Airports

4)

I, Rearrangement Servant // "Dying Earth Genre"

Entry to elsewhere. Where
    were you last night?

The earnest stigma in the house.

Where were you last night?
    Sheltering

in the theater / in the garden
    under the edge of water

in a tunnel of honey
    in the highway hour

it is early to be dying.

Entry to Remington Theory:
    Integral minstrel, our gang

the senate! You dynamite sluggers.
    Dying tiger, meet dying rose.

In greenhouse denial, gold rhymes
    with orange, gold rhymes

with lash. Gold rhymes with ruin,
    gold rhymes with ash.

It's tee time: return to Eden
    with a golem in the gears.

Right on, angel. This earth
    somehow leaner.

5)

- Downtown
- Paris
- London
- Parades

- Lunch hour
- Conferences
- Airplanes
- Museums

- Landmarks
- Towers
- Tunnels
- Popular beaches

6)

I stand in a room with windows too heavy to open,
too high to jump from, and point to a poem
on the blackboard. I point to lines about boys

throwing rocks *at the head of the burned girl*, circle
the adjectives and say *here is where the specificity
of the description heightens the stakes, makes the violence*

*believable. Now the act is vicious, the perpetrators: more
vicious still.* In a poem my student writes, the fired
bullet *nestles*. Bullet as habituation, habitation. The

room is in a small liberal arts college at the foot
of a forest so wild it won't condescend to cell
phone signals. I see now how young they are,

these students, ill dressed for the weather. It is fall
and the light from these windows behaves as
you'd expect: it rushes in. It strangles.

7)

I, Rearrangement Servant // "Golem in the Gears"

Disgorgement (law): Dailystrength.org
English gardener dangerous when wet.
Team triggers down, dragnet
(theme song). Angel on the right, enlightened rogue.
High desert league determining growth.
Our gang (the shield) duel in the senate.
Dynamite wrestler see-through-garment,
largemouth sinner arguing the world.

General interest: where were you last night.
Anywhere in the world. Hemingway:
on the edge. Enter the demon.
Three minute wonder, where were you last night?
Otherwise engaged. Ernest Hemingway,
Great white wonder. Return to Eden
    (the game).

8)

- School
- School
- School
- School

- School
- School
- School
- School

- School
- School
- School
- School

9)

*I, Rearrangement Servant // "When Times
    Were Hard in the Mother's Land"*

The Dog in the Manger
    The Golden Treasury
Legendary Twins
    The Golden Earrings
The Miner's Daughter
    The Rose and the Ring
Miners Daughters
    The Rose and the Rime
Under the Water Line

The Daily Southerner
    The Whole Nine Yards
The Great Hog Swindle
    Lady in the Morgue
The Grime and the Glow
    Underlying Theme:

You're with Me, Leather
    Angel with the Sword

10)

My friend's three-year-old son
    has a dollbaby. The dollbaby's name
is Pete. Holding Pete under his arm,
    Pete's hand is the trigger
& the bullets come out of Pete's feet.

Pete is a gun, he says. *Blam blam.*
    Pete is a gun blam blam.

The phrase "I, Rearrangement Servant" is an inexact anagram of "they were armed with long guns." The words and phrases of parts 4, 7, and 10 are inexact anagrams of "they were armed with long guns." They are inexact because the phrases are formed from the same letters, in a different order, but the letters are occasionally repeated. The phrase "they were armed with long guns" was pulled from a news article on CNN about a mass shooting.

I BELIEVE THE FAR FIELDS ARE MADE OF GLASS

& research. Corn clad & thick on moans. There at the edge of the wheel the tar bubbles burst and they kept on bursting as long as the mile stayed a mile which it did. What they did not want to speak of, the men burned out there: pasture, polio rags, poplin junk as long as there was a day to foul which was a long while. Tar a wincing mammal. Someone asked if I missed my friends. The more erotic pints we shared. But I squeezed & pulled one damp loaf down from the shelf after another. Donning a mania all his own, Teddy Roosevelt believed in boar hunts and war-suckled men. He'd have something to say about this enterprising sunset, the shivering alfalfa, trim and sweet like champagne.

NEGATIVE MONEY

So delirious from drought
    my town went singing
to seeds. Those who stayed

could barely make a Sunday
    choir. Not enough juice
in the county to plump up

the memory of water, or a single
    itinerant tomato. I made
the same poisoned meal.

Days like two midnights in a jar
    and it takes twice as much
money to live the way a cactus

lives on air. My men
    took to cards & drink
as punishment for stricken soil.

The dust blew so bad
    and like anyone I made a list
of names I wouldn't mind dressing

in a child of my own. We paid
    a charlatan to shoot rain
out of clouds but the dynamite

tied to kites proved more useless
    than mud. Like any good charlatan
he never returned.

Enough pale misery. Now we are
    poor in every corner
of the word. Not a pot to piss in,

or skin of a fig to suck on.

I OFTEN FALL ASLEEP WITH ONE EARRING IN MY EAR

The left stud burrows into me
& I dream we ride together in a Subaru
      to the county fair where we eat bloodied applies
      and funnels of powdered dough. You are my ex-lover dangling
from the swings. Or maybe we are still lovers
and I suck on your long hair snarled with sugars. Our boots
      shine and sweaters crisp and nearby a seashore strums,
      sings on about its gold coins, about whom christened
the lighthouse for whom.

      Outside how I really live
this life is so white and the sun smartens our darling cheeks.
The oysters come to us, bellies pinched
on buttered stones. The bodies I gave, you never tongued,
      never truly received. Your sex couldn't come
with honest desire. The pigs route & topple
the grandstands and all the words for *flannel* are exhausted
by the season's endless invocation of a return to pure
      pictures of home.

The color of the sea is the color of paint we paint
      our cottage to look like the sea—the last place we choose
to live is always where we plan to die. I roll over to a stabbing
      & rise out of the wind as it blows towards me
a coastal state full of cliffs.

MAINE COAST

I watch the ocean square into a turning

Burn. Burning, my holes glass over. Lightning

Hits the beach, melts me shut. I've drowned

Before, in the bye along a row of shored

Rocks. From the barrel chest butcher I buy

Tight roasts. This year's man, his clownish dog walks me

In the park until I die on its leash and domestic

Night's sticky seizures. I thumb and ♥ it

Like liking a million times. The rich own long

Lighthouses to show us how away from them

We are. Past waiting for the press of his chest

To my back, I hobby along to the next hem's

Promise. Again I straddle the blade thinking

This is the time it will fill the gash.

FACTS ABOUT DEER

Because this is a still a poem with an animal in it
and I am still trying—I might say "it offers you
its meaty heart, with no lasting conditions."

If you've seen a struck deer thrash its life out
on the shoulder, a burner that clicks
without flaming, you know how they seize to death.

Who cares what I think, but I wished just then
to have a knife. I wished I knew a little about guns
and to own one or to know something sorcerous.

Because nothing but blood tastes like blood, I've cut
myself for its coppery flavor. *Only God knows
I'm good.* My mother says I've no scruples, the way

I make no claims to being a permanent person,
how my move from husband to ex-husband came on
a wave of expediency and self-promotion. If you've gone

to the store and left behind a life—the kind that comes
with seating, spare change jars, someone's green thumb
—then you know how I angered at the woman

shrieking behind the wheel of her cracked Ford Escape,
phone to face, doe spasming on the shoulder.
Someone should knuckle up and kill this deer. A roadway

in America and there's no policeman on hand to squash
a neck? It's early evening & the sky's poetically
blameless gray fills your throat with the thick despair

so familiar to the heavily indebted. Mountaineers know
you can't save anyone on good will, that high altitude
is minus morality. So, Confessionalism. Or,

Two Truths and a Lie: I married a man I met
on an airplane. I killed that deer. I have no patience
for even the most cherubic of children.

HUSBAND STORIES

a computationally mediated poem

[8]

I speak to no one from that past....My silence put to use
is the highest instrument....Now even the frost holds my
hand...I got rid of the life....It took all the *n*s to make a no.
...The distance is here....As for the chandelier......I
dig a well....Into the well I put many men.

[7]

There was a husband in the center of this story....Some
lunar waves were ringing....I got rid of the husband....
Even my ankle rejects you!...I never told anyone,
not really....The distance is here....Light in a circle
could not save me.

[6]

Even the light has aged.…The story does not compute.
…Some lunar waves were ringing.…My silence put to use,
its highest instrument.…Now even the frost holds my
hand.…The things lost with many traces.…I dig a well.
…Into the well I put many men.…There are rows of
waiting others.

[5]

I speak to no one from that past.…Some lunar waves were
ringing.…What is left of leaves are stone.…Now even
the frost holds my hand.…I got rid of the life.
…If I could take it all back.…It took all the *n*s to
make a no.…Into the well I put many men.…That husband
is gone.…There are rows of waiting others.

[4]

The story does not compute....There is a husband in the center of this story....What is left of leaves are stone. ...If I could take it all back....Even my ankle rejects you!...The distance is here....The ear up close.

[3]

The story does not compute....My silence put to use, its highest instrument....If I could take it all back....Even my ankle rejects you!...I never told anyone, not really. ...It took all the *n*s to make a no....The distance is here....Light in a circle could not save me....I dig a well....Into the well I put many men.

[2]

The story does not compute....there is a husband in the center of this story....My silence put to use, its highest instrument....I got rid of the husband....The distance is here....The ear up close....Light in a circle could not save me....I dig a well....That husband is gone....There are rows of waiting others.

[1]

Even the light has aged....Some lunar waves were ringing.
...My silence put to use is its highest instrument....What is
left of leaves are stone....Real gaps spread in the tropic
of paradise....If I could take it all back....I never told
anyone, not really....The things lost without traces.
...It took all the *n*s to make a no....I dig a well.

GEORGIC

I wake in another country and crumple the fuel.
The air whines with accelerant. Ahead the marble portico
is an arcade of cool fire. I've misplaced my eyes
in the girl whose boy winds whalebone and won't leave her alone.
Lifelike I step into the next country where it is too late
to summon the czar now a thimble of ash. On the last tide
every masted boat is leaving and not a single shop will open
to sell me my missing clothes.

ACKNOWLEDGMENTS

"Husband Stories":

The Python code is adapted from Nick Montfort's "Through the Park" code (#!, Counterpath 2014). This code generates stories by randomly omitting different sentences from a prepared list through each iteration. The output has been edited and arranged. Nick's implementation and the code can be found in #! and on his website:

> http://nickm.com/poems/through_the_park.py

The poem referenced in section 6 of "They were armed with long guns" is "The Blue Terrance" by Terrance Hayes.

Grateful acknowledgment is given to the publications in which these poems, in some form, appeared: *The Account: A Journal of Poetry and Prose*, *Bennington Review*, *Figure 1*, *Narrative Magazine*, *Nepantla*, and *The Walrus*.

To Anne Marie Rooney, for everything.

LILLIAN-YVONNE BERTRAM is the author of *Personal Science* (Tupelo Press), *a slice from the cake made of air* (Red Hen Press), *But a Storm is Blowing From Paradise* (chosen by Claudia Rankine as winner of the 2010 Red Hen Press Benjamin Saltman Award), the chapbook *cutthroat glamour* (Phantom Books), and the artist book *Grand Dessein* (Container). As of this writing Lillian-Yvonne Bertram resides in Massachusetts and teaches in the MFA program at UMass-Boston.

❈

COLOPHON

Text is set in a digital version of Jenson, designed by Robert Slimbach in 1996, and based on the work of punchcutter, printer, and publisher Nicolas Jenson. The titles here are in Futura.

❉

NEW MICHIGAN PRESS, based in Tucson, Arizona, prints poetry and prose chapbooks, especially work that transcends traditional genre. Together with *DIAGRAM*, NMP sponsors a yearly chapbook competition.

DIAGRAM, a journal of text, art, and schematic, is published bimonthly at THEDIAGRAM.COM. Periodic print anthologies are available from the New Michigan Press at NEWMICHIGANPRESS.COM.

www.ingramcontent.com/pod-product-compliance
Lightning Source LLC
Chambersburg PA
CBHW031505040426
42444CB00007B/1214